# UNDERSTANDING THE IMPORTANCE OF AUTHORITY

## Biblical and Practical Approaches to Victory

# UNDERSTANDING THE IMPORTANCE OF AUTHORITY

Biblical and Practical Approaches to Victory

*Compiled by* Eugene Carvalho

*To the Body of Christ.*
*May this compilation bless you richly!*
*With love…*

# TABLE OF CONTENTS

# PURPOSE AND ACKNOWLEDGEMENTS

The infallible Word of God for faith and conduct informs us that the Holy Spirit gives gifts to men and women of the Body of Christ. It states: "the gifts edify the body for the building up of the saints" (Eph. 4:12). I hope the talents and gifts the Lord has given me will be a blessing to someone else through the reading of this compilation.

I am grateful for the love from all family members, especially my wife Mercedes Carvalho. I am also grateful for the knowledge, wisdom and love of many pastors, teachers, and saints that the Lord has used to bless me. Lastly, I must not forget a special thank you to my friend Kathryn Regan for proofreading this material.

# UNDERSTANDING THE IMPORTANCE OF AUTHORITY

It's crucial you understand everywhere you go God has established authority you need to submit to. Wives submit to your husbands. Children submit to your parents. Employees submit to your employer. Shoppers' submit to the person at the cash register. Drivers submit to the speed limit. Ushers submit to your pastor.

When an individual does not submit to God's authority it's called rebellion. The Bible says, "For rebellion is as the sin of witchcraft, and stubbornness is as iniquity and idolatry" (1 Sam. 15:23 KJV).

Submitting to God's authority is one thing. Taking the authority God has given you as a believer is another matter. Understand God gave all authority to Adam, and when he sinned, he gave that authority to Satan. The good news is Jesus was victorious over Satan, sin, death, and the grave. He rose on the third day and gave authority back to every born-again believer. Now that you're born-again the kingdom of God is within you. Satan no longer has power over you. He can only deceive, condemn, and tempt you. The only power he has is the power you give him. You give Satan power when you speak wrong. He deceives you to get you to speak wrongly. Your victory is in your authority that is in your mouth. It's vital to speak bold declarations of faith and run Satan and the kingdom of darkness out of town, in Jesus' name!

Jesus gave the authority back to every born-again believer. The Bibles says, "Then he called his twelve disciples together, and gave them power and authority over all devils, and to cure diseases. And he sent them to preach the kingdom of God, and to heal the sick" (Lk. 9:1-2).[1] Also, "Behold, I give unto you power to tread on serpents and scorpions, and over all the power of the enemy: and nothing shall by any means hurt you" (Lk. 10:19 KJV).

This is why it's vital to meditate on the Word day and night. "Faith comes by hearing and by hearing the Word of God" (Ro. 10:17). Your faith filled words and authority are going to get you your next victory which will be today, in Jesus' name. Words of faith connect you to God and His blessings and words of fear connect you to Satan and his curses.

Most important is the baptism of the Holy Spirit. The Bible says, "...You shall receive power when the Holy Spirit has come upon you; and you shall be My witnesses both in Jerusalem, and in all Judea and Samaria, and even to the remotest part of the earth" (Acts 1:8). The Baptism of the Holy Spirit is enablement and empowerment for service and witnessing.

The purpose of this compilation is to have the scriptures give you fresh revelation and insight concerning authority which in turn will lead you to victory after victory.

---

[1] All Scripture quotations, unless otherwise noted, are from the *New American Standard Bible*.

# AUTHORITY IN THE OLD TESTAMENT

## IN THE BOOK OF GENESIS

### Return to Your Mistress, and Submit Yourself to Her Authority

"Now the angel of the Lord found her by a spring of water in the wilderness, by the spring on the way to Shur. He said, 'Hagar, Sarai's maid, where have you come from and where are you going?' And she said, 'I am fleeing from the presence of my mistress Sarai.' Then the angel of the Lord said to her, 'Return to your mistress, and submit yourself to her authority.' Moreover, the angel of the Lord said to her, 'I will greatly multiply your descendants so that they will be too many to count.' The angel of the Lord said to her further, 'Behold, you are with child, and you will bear a son; and you shall call his name Ishmael, because the Lord has given heed to your affliction. He will be a wild donkey of a man, His hand will be against everyone, and everyone's hand will be against him; and he will live to the east of all his brothers. Then she called the name of the Lord who spoke to her, 'You are a God who sees'; for she said, 'Have I even remained alive here after seeing Him?' Therefore the well was called Beer-lahai-roi; behold, it is between Kadesh and Bered" (Ge. 16:7-14).

## Under Pharaoh's Authority

"Now Joseph said to Pharaoh, 'Pharaoh's dreams are one and the same; God has told to Pharaoh what He is about to do. The seven good cows are seven years; and the seven good ears are seven years; the dreams are one and the same. The seven lean and ugly cows that came up after them are seven years, and the seven thin ears scorched by the east wind will be seven years of famine. It is as I have spoken to Pharaoh: God has shown to Pharaoh what He is about to do. Behold, seven years of great abundance are coming in all the land of Egypt; and after them seven years of famine will come, and all the abundance will be forgotten in the land of Egypt, and the famine will ravage the land. So the abundance will be unknown in the land because of that subsequent famine; for it will be very severe. Now as for the repeating of the dream to Pharaoh twice, it means that the matter is determined by God, and God will quickly bring it about. Now let Pharaoh look for a man discerning and wise, and set him over the land of Egypt. Let Pharaoh take action to appoint overseers in charge of the land, and let him exact a fifth of the produce of the land of Egypt in the seven years of abundance. Then let them gather all the food of these good years that are coming, and store up the grain for food in the cities under Pharaoh's authority, and let them guard it. Let the food become as a reserve for the land for the seven years of famine which will occur in the land of Egypt, so that the land will not perish during the famine'" (Ge. 41:25-36).

## IN THE BOOK OF EXODUS

### He Does Not Have Authority to Sell Her

"If a man sells his daughter as a female slave, she is not to go free as the male slaves do. If she is displeasing in the eyes of her master who designated her for himself, then he shall let her be redeemed. He does not have authority to sell her to a foreign people because of his unfairness to her. If he designates her for his son, he shall deal with her according to the custom of daughters. If he takes to himself another woman, he may not reduce her food, her clothing, or her conjugal rights. If he will not do these three things for her, then she shall go out for nothing, without payment of money" (Ex. 21:7-11).

## IN THE BOOK OF NUMBERS

### Being Under the Authority of Your Husband

"Then the priest shall bring her near and have her stand before the Lord, and the priest shall take holy water in an earthenware vessel; and he shall take some of the dust that is on the floor of the tabernacle and put it into the water. The priest shall then have the woman stand before the Lord and let the hair of the woman's head go loose, and place the grain offering of memorial in her hands, which is the grain offering of jealousy, and in the hand of the priest is to be the water of bitterness that brings a curse. The priest shall have her take an oath and shall say to the woman, 'If no man has lain with you and if you have not gone astray into uncleanness, being under the authority of your husband, be immune to this water of bitterness that brings a curse; if you, however, have gone astray, being under the authority of your husband, and if you have defiled yourself and a man other than your husband has had intercourse with you (then the priest shall have the woman swear with the oath of the curse, and the priest shall say to the woman), the Lord make you a curse and an oath among your people by the Lord's making your thigh waste away and your abdomen swell; and this water that brings a curse shall go into your stomach, and make your abdomen swell and your thigh waste away.' And the woman shall say, 'Amen. Amen'" (Nu. 5:16-22).

## Under the Authority of Her Husband, Goes Astray

"This is the law of jealousy: when a wife, being under the authority of her husband, goes astray and defiles herself, or when a spirit of jealousy comes over a man and he is jealous of his wife, he shall then make the woman stand before the Lord, and the priest shall apply all this law to her. Moreover, the man will be free from guilt, but that woman shall bear her guilt'" (Nu. 5:29-31).

## You Shall Put Some of Your Authority on Him

"Then Moses spoke to the Lord, saying, 'May the Lord, the God of the spirits of all flesh, appoint a man over the congregation, who will go out and come in before them, and who will lead them out and bring them in, so that the congregation of the Lord will not be like sheep which have no shepherd.' So the Lord said to Moses, 'Take Joshua the son of Nun, a man in whom is the Spirit, and lay your hand on him; and have him stand before Eleazar the priest and before all the congregation, and commission him in their sight. You shall put some of your authority on him, in order that all the congregation of the sons of Israel may obey him. Moreover, he shall stand before Eleazar the priest, who shall inquire for him by the judgment of the Urim before the Lord. At his command they shall go out and at his command they shall come in, both he and the sons of Israel with him, even all the congregation. Moses did just as the Lord commanded him; and he took Joshua and set him before Eleazar the priest and before all the congregation. Then he laid his hands on him and commissioned him, just as the Lord had spoken through Moses'" (Nu. 27:15-23).

# IN THE BOOK OF JUDGES

## This People Were Under My Authority

"Now Gaal the son of Ebed came with his relatives, and crossed over into Shechem; and the men of Shechem put their trust in him. They went out into the field and gathered the grapes of their vineyards and trod them, and held a festival; and they went into the house of their god, and ate and drank and cursed Abimelech. Then Gaal the son of Ebed said, 'Who is Abimelech, and who is Shechem, that we should serve him? Is he not the son of Jerubbaal, and is Zebul not his lieutenant? Serve the men of Hamor the father of Shechem; but why should we serve him? Would, therefore, that this people were under my authority! Then I would remove Abimelech. And he said to Abimelech, 'Increase your army and come out'" (Jdg. 9:26-29).

# IN THE BOOK OF 2 CHRONICLES

## Under the Authority of the Levitical Priests

"Then Jehoiada made a covenant between himself and all the people and the king, that they would be the Lord's people. And all the people went to the house of Baal and tore it down, and they broke in pieces his altars and his images, and killed Mattan the priest of Baal before the altars. Moreover, Jehoiada placed the offices of the house of the Lord under the authority of the Levitical priests, whom David had assigned over the house of the Lord, to offer the burnt offerings of the Lord, as it is written in the law of Moses — with rejoicing and singing according to the order of David. He stationed the gatekeepers of the house of the Lord, so that no one would enter who was in any way unclean. He took the captains of hundreds, the nobles, the rulers of the people and all the people of the land, and brought the king down from the house of the Lord, and came through the upper gate to the king's house. And they placed the king upon the royal throne. So all of the people of the land rejoiced and the city was quiet. For they had put Athaliah to death with the sword" (2Ch. 23:16-21).

## Were Overseers Under the Authority
## of Conaniah

"Then Hezekiah commanded them to prepare rooms in the house of the Lord, and they prepared them. They faithfully brought in the contributions and the tithes and the consecrated things; and Conaniah the Levite was the officer in charge of them and his brother Shimei was second. Jehiel, Azaziah, Nahath, Asahel, Jerimoth, Jozabad, Eliel, Ismachiah, Mahath and Benaiah were overseers under the authority of Conaniah and Shimei his brother by the appointment of King Hezekiah, and Azariah was the chief officer of the house of God. Kore the son of Imnah the

Levite, the keeper of the eastern gate, was over the freewill offerings of God, to apportion the contributions for the Lord and the most holy things. Under his authority were Eden, Miniamin, Jeshua, Shemaiah, Amariah and Shecaniah in the cities of the priests, to distribute faithfully their portions to their brothers by divisions, whether great or small, without regard to their genealogical enrollment, to the males from thirty years old and upward—everyone who entered the house of the Lord for his daily obligations—for their work in their duties according to their divisions; as well as the priests who were enrolled genealogically according to their fathers' households, and the Levites from twenty years old and upwards, by their duties and their divisions. The genealogical enrollment included all their little children, their wives, their sons and their daughters, for the whole assembly, for they consecrated themselves faithfully in holiness. Also for the sons of Aaron the priests who were in the pasture lands of their cities, or in each and every city, there were men who were designated by name to distribute portions to every male among the priests and to everyone genealogically enrolled among the Levites" (2Ch. 31:11-19).

# IN THE BOOK OF ESTHER

## Advanced Him and Established His Authority Over All the Princes

"After these events King Ahasuerus promoted Haman, the son of Hammedatha the Agagite, and advanced him and established his authority over all the princes who were with him. All the king's servants who were at the king's gate bowed down and paid homage to Haman; for so the king had commanded concerning him. But Mordecai neither bowed down nor paid homage. Then the king's servants who were at the king's gate said to Mordecai, 'Why are you transgressing the king's command?' Now it was when they had spoken daily to him and he would not listen to them, that they told Haman to see whether Mordecai's reason would stand; for he had told them that he was a Jew. When Haman saw that Mordecai neither bowed down nor paid homage to him, Haman was filled with rage. But he disdained to lay hands on Mordecai alone, for they had told him who the people of Mordecai were; therefore Haman sought to destroy all the Jews, the people of Mordecai, who were throughout the whole kingdom of Ahasuerus" (Est. 3:1-6).

*Chapter Two*

# Wrote with Authority to Confirm this Second Letter

"Then Queen Esther, daughter of Abihail, with Mordecai the Jew, wrote with full authority to confirm this second letter about Purim. He sent letters to all the Jews, to the 127 provinces of the kingdom of Ahasuerus, namely, words of peace and truth, to establish these days of Purim at their appointed times, just as Mordecai the Jew and Queen Esther had established for them, and just as they had established for themselves and for their descendants with instructions for their times of fasting and their lamentations. The command of Esther established these customs for Purim, and it was written in the book" (Est. 9:29-32).

## All the Accomplishments of His Authority and Strength

"Now King Ahasuerus laid a tribute on the land and on the coastlands of the sea. And all the accomplishments of his authority and strength, and the full account of the greatness of Mordecai to which the king advanced him, are they not written in the Book of the Chronicles of the Kings of Media and Persia? For Mordecai the Jew was second only to King Ahasuerus, and great among the Jews and in favor with his many kinsmen, one who sought the good of his people and one who spoke for the welfare of his whole nation" (Est. 10:1-3).

# IN THE BOOK OF JOB

## Who Gave Him Authority over the Earth

"Therefore, listen to me, you men of understanding. Far be it from God to do wickedness, And from the Almighty to do wrong. For He pays a man according to his work, And makes him find it according to his way. Surely, God will not act wickedly, And the Almighty will not pervert justice. Who gave Him authority over the earth? And who has laid on Him the whole world? If He should determine to do so, If He should gather to Himself His spirit and His breath, All flesh would perish together, And man would return to dust" (Job 34:10-15).

# IN THE BOOK OF ECCLESIASTES

## No Man Has Authority to Restrain the Wind

"He who keeps a royal command experiences no trouble, for a wise heart knows the proper time and procedure. For there is a proper time and procedure for every delight, though a man's trouble is heavy upon him. If no one knows what will happen, who can tell him when it will happen? No man has authority to restrain the wind with the wind, or authority over the day of death; and there is no discharge in the time of war, and evil will not deliver those who practice it.  All this I have seen and applied my mind to every deed that has been done under the sun wherein a man has exercised authority over another man to his hurt" (Ecc. 8:5-9).

## IN THE BOOK OF ISAIAH

### I Will Entrust Him with Your Authority

"Thus says the Lord God of hosts, 'Come, go to this steward, To Shebna, who is in charge of the royal household, "What right do you have here, And whom do you have here, That you have hewn a tomb for yourself here, You who hew a tomb on the height, You who carve a resting place for yourself in the rock? Behold, the Lord is about to hurl you headlong, O man. And He is about to grasp you firmly And roll you tightly like a ball, To be cast into a vast country; There you will die And there your splendid chariots will be, You shame of your master's house." I will depose you from your office, And I will pull you down from your station. Then it will come about in that day, That I will summon My servant Eliakim the son of Hilkiah, And I will clothe him with your tunic And tie your sash securely about him. I will entrust him with your authority, And he will become a father to the inhabitants of Jerusalem and to the house of Judah. Then I will set the key of the house of David on his shoulder, When he opens no one will shut, When he shuts no one will open. I will drive him like a peg in a firm place, And he will become a throne of glory to his father's house. So they will hang on him all the glory of his father's house, offspring and issue, all the least of vessels, from bowls to all the jars. In that day,' declares the Lord of hosts, 'the peg driven in a firm place will give way; it will even break off and fall, and the load hanging on it will be cut off, for the Lord has spoken'" (Is. 22:15-25).

## Will Cause His Voice of Authority to be Heard

"Behold, the name of the Lord comes from a remote place; Burning is His anger and dense is His smoke; His lips are filled with indignation And His tongue is like a consuming fire; His breath is like an overflowing torrent, Which reaches to the neck, To shake the nations back and forth in a sieve, And to put in the jaws of the peoples the bridle which leads to ruin. You will have songs as in the night when you keep the festival, And gladness of heart as when one marches to the sound of the flute, To go to the mountain of the Lord, to the Rock of Israel. And the Lord will cause His voice of authority to be heard, And the descending of His arm to be seen in fierce anger, And in the flame of a consuming fire In cloudburst, downpour and hailstones. For at the voice of the Lord Assyria will be terrified, When He strikes with the rod. And every blow of the rod of punishment, Which the Lord will lay on him, Will be with the music of tambourines and lyres; And in battles, brandishing weapons, He will fight them. For Topheth has long been ready,

Indeed, it has been prepared for the king. He has made it deep and large, A pyre of fire with plenty of wood; The breath of the Lord, like a torrent of brimstone, sets it afire" (Is. 30:27-33).

## IN THE BOOK OF JEREMIAH

### The Priests Rule on their Own Authority

"An appalling and horrible thing Has happened in the land: The prophets prophesy falsely, And the priests rule on their own authority; And My people love it so! But what will you do at the end of it" (Jer. 5:30-31)?

### Take Thirty Men from Here Under Your Authority

"Now Shephatiah the son of Mattan, and Gedaliah the son of Pashhur, and Jucal the son of Shelemiah, and Pashhur the son of Malchijah heard the words that Jeremiah was speaking to all the people, saying, 'Thus says the Lord, "He who stays in this city will die by the sword and by famine and by pestilence, but he who goes out to the Chaldeans will live and have his own life as booty and stay alive." Thus says the Lord, "This city will certainly be given into the hand of the army of the king of Babylon and he will capture it."' Then the officials said to the king, 'Now let this man be put to death, inasmuch as he is discouraging the men of war who are left in this city and all the people, by speaking such words to them; for this man is not seeking the well-being of this people but rather their harm.' So King Zedekiah said, 'Behold, he is in your hands; for the king can do nothing against you.' Then they took Jeremiah and cast him into the cistern of Malchijah the king's son, which was in the court of the guardhouse; and they let Jeremiah down with ropes. Now in the cistern there was no water but only mud, and Jeremiah sank into the mud. But Ebed-melech the Ethiopian, a eunuch, while he was in the king's palace, heard that they had put Jeremiah into the cistern. Now the king was sitting in the Gate of Benjamin; and Ebed-melech went out from the king's palace and spoke to the king, saying, 'My lord the king, these men have acted wickedly in all that they have done to Jeremiah the prophet whom they have cast into the cistern; and he will die right where he is because of the famine, for there is no more bread in the city.' Then the king commanded Ebed-melech the Ethiopian, saying, 'Take thirty men from here under your authority and bring up Jeremiah the prophet from the cistern before he dies.' So Ebed-melech took the men under his authority and went into the king's palace to a place beneath the storeroom and took from there worn-out clothes and worn-out rags and let them down by ropes into the cistern to Jeremiah. Then Ebed-melech the Ethiopian said to Jeremiah, 'Now put these worn-out clothes and rags under your armpits under the ropes'; and Jeremiah did so. So they pulled Jeremiah up with the ropes and lifted him out of the cistern, and Jeremiah stayed in the court of the guardhouse" (Jer. 38:1-13).

## IN THE BOOK OF DANIEL

### Have Authority as Third Ruler in the Kingdom

"Suddenly the fingers of a man's hand emerged and began writing opposite the lampstand on the plaster of the wall of the king's palace, and the king saw the back of the hand that did the writing. Then the king's face grew pale and his thoughts alarmed him, and his hip joints went slack and his knees began knocking together. The king called aloud to bring in the conjurers, the Chaldeans and the diviners. The king spoke and said to the wise men of Babylon, 'Any man who can read this inscription and explain its interpretation to me shall be clothed with purple and have a necklace of gold around his neck, and have authority as third ruler in the kingdom.' Then all the king's wise men came in, but they could not read the inscription or make known its interpretation to the king. Then King Belshazzar was greatly alarmed, his face grew even paler, and his nobles were perplexed" (Da. 5:5-9).

### You Will Have Authority

"Then Daniel was brought in before the king. The king spoke and said to Daniel, 'Are you that Daniel who is one of the exiles from Judah, whom my father the king brought from Judah? Now I have heard about you that a spirit of the gods is in you, and that illumination, insight and extraordinary wisdom have been found in you. Just now the wise men and the conjurers were brought in before me that they might read this inscription and make its interpretation known to me, but they could not declare the interpretation of the message. But I personally have heard about you, that you are able to give interpretations and solve difficult problems. Now if you are able to read the inscription and make its interpretation known to me, you will be clothed with purple and wear a necklace of gold around your neck, and you will have authority as the third ruler in the kingdom'" (Da. 5:13-16).

## A Proclamation Concerning Him That He Now Had Authority

"Then Belshazzar gave orders, and they clothed Daniel with purple and put a necklace of gold around his neck, and issued a proclamation concerning him that he now had authority as the third ruler in the kingdom" (Da. 5:29).

## Nor According to His Authority Which He Wielded

"In the first year of Darius the Mede, I arose to be an encouragement and a protection for him.

And now I will tell you the truth. Behold, three more kings are going to arise in Persia. Then a fourth will gain far more riches than all of them;as soon as he becomes strong through his riches, he will arouse the whole empire against the realm of Greece. And a mighty king will arise, and he will rule with great authority and do as he pleases. But as soon as he has arisen, his kingdom will be broken up and parceled out toward the four points of the compass, though not to his own descendants, nor according to his authority which he wielded, for his sovereignty will be uprooted and given to others besides them" (Da. 11:1-4).

## IN THE BOOK OF HABAKKUK

### Their Justice and Authority Originate with Themselves

"Look among the nations! Observe! Be astonished! Wonder! Because I am doing something in your days — You would not believe if you were told. For behold, I am raising up the Chaldeans, That fierce and impetuous people Who march throughout the earth To seize dwelling places which are not theirs. They are dreaded and feared; Their justice and authority originate with themselves. Their horses are swifter than leopards And keener than wolves in the evening. Their horsemen come galloping, Their horsemen come from afar; They fly like an eagle swooping down to devour. All of them come for violence. Their horde of faces moves forward. They collect captives like sand. They mock at kings And rulers are a laughing matter to them. They laugh at every fortress And heap up rubble to capture it. Then they will sweep through like the wind and pass on. But they will be held guilty, They whose strength is their god" (Hab.1:5-11).

# AUTHORITY IN THE NEW TESTAMENT

## IN THE BOOK OF MATTHEW

## He was Teaching Them as One Having Authority

"When Jesus had finished these words, the crowds were amazed at His teaching; for He was teaching them as one having authority, and not as their scribes" (Mt. 7:28-29).

## I Also Am a Man Under Authority

"And when Jesus entered Capernaum, a centurion came to Him, imploring Him, and saying, 'Lord, my servant is lying paralyzed at home, fearfully tormented.' Jesus said to him, 'I will come and heal him.' But the centurion said, 'Lord, I am not worthy for You to come under my roof, but just say the word, and my servant will be healed. For I also am a man under authority, with soldiers under me; and I say to this one, "Go!" and he goes, and to another, "Come!" and he comes, and to my slave, "Do this!" and he does it.' Now when Jesus heard this, He marveled and said to those who were following, 'Truly I say to you, I have not found such great faith with anyone in Israel. "I say to you that many will come from east and west, and recline at the table with Abraham, Isaac and Jacob in the kingdom of heaven; but the sons of the kingdom will be cast out into the outer darkness; in that place there will be weeping and gnashing of teeth.' And Jesus said to the centurion, 'Go; it shall be done for you as you have believed.' And the servant was healed that very moment" (Mt. 8:5-13).

## The Son of Man Has Authority on Earth to Forgive Sins

"And they brought to Him a paralytic lying on a bed. Seeing their faith, Jesus said to the paralytic, 'Take courage, son; your sins are forgiven.' And some of the scribes said to themselves, 'This fellow blasphemes.' And Jesus knowing their thoughts said, 'Why are you thinking evil in your hearts? Which is easier, to say, "Your sins are forgiven," or to say, "Get up, and walk"? But so that you may know that the Son of Man has authority on earth to forgive sins" — then He said to the paralytic, 'Get up, pick up your bed and go home.' And he got up and went home. But when the crowds saw this, they were awestruck, and glorified God, who had given such authority to men" (Mt. 9:2-8).

## His Twelve Disciples and Gave Them Authority Over Unclean Spirits

"Jesus summoned His twelve disciples and gave them authority over unclean spirits, to cast them out, and to heal every kind of disease and every kind of sickness" (Mt. 10:1).

*Chapter Three*

## Their Great Men Exercise Authority over Them

"And hearing this, the ten became indignant with the two brothers. But Jesus called them to Himself and said, 'You know that the rulers of the Gentiles lord it over them, and their great men exercise authority over them. It is not this way among you, but whoever wishes to become great among you shall be your servant, and whoever wishes to be first among you shall be your slave; just as the Son of Man did not come to be served, but to serve, and to give His life a ransom for many'" (Mt. 20:24-28).

## By What Authority Are You Doing These Things

"When He entered the temple, the chief priests and the elders of the people came to Him while He was teaching, and said, 'By what authority are You doing these things, and who gave You this authority?' Jesus said to them, 'I will also ask you one thing, which if you tell Me, I will also tell you by what authority I do these things. The baptism of John was from what source, from heaven or from men?' And they began reasoning among themselves, saying, 'If we say, "From heaven," He will say to us, "Then why did you not believe him?" But if we say, "From men," we fear the people; for they all regard John as a prophet.' And answering Jesus, they said, 'We do not know.' He also said to them, "Neither will I tell you by what authority I do these things'" (Mt. 21:23-27).

## All Authority Has Been Given to Me

"But the eleven disciples proceeded to Galilee, to the mountain which Jesus had designated. When they saw Him, they worshiped Him;but some were doubtful. And Jesus came up and spoke to them, saying, 'All authority has been given to Me in heaven and on earth. Go therefore and make disciples of all the nations, baptizing them in the name of the Father and the Son and the Holy Spirit,  teaching them to observe all that I commanded you; and lo, I am with you always, even to the end of the age'" (Mt. 28:16-20).

## IN THE BOOK OF MARK

## He Was Teaching Them as One Having Authority

"They went into Capernaum; and immediately on the Sabbath He entered the synagogue and began to teach. They were amazed at His teaching; for He was teaching them as one having authority, and not as the scribes. Just then there was a man in their synagogue with an unclean spirit; and he cried out, saying, 'What business do we have with each other, Jesus of Nazareth? Have You come to destroy us? I know who You are — the Holy One of God!' And Jesus rebuked him, saying, 'Be quiet, and come out of him!' Throwing him into convulsions, the unclean spirit cried out with a loud voice and came out of him. They were all amazed, so that they debated among themselves, saying, 'What is this? A new teaching with authority! He commands even the unclean spirits, and they obey Him.' Immediately the news about Him spread everywhere into all the surrounding district of Galilee" (Mk. 1:21-28).

## The Son of Man has Authority on Earth

"When He had come back to Capernaum several days afterward, it was heard that He was at home. And many were gathered together, so that there was no longer room, not even near the door; and He was speaking the word to them. And they came, bringing to Him a paralytic, carried by four men. Being unable to get to Him because of the crowd, they removed the roof above Him; and when they had dug an opening, they let down the pallet on which the paralytic was lying. And Jesus seeing their faith said to the paralytic, 'Son, your sins are forgiven.' But some of the scribes were sitting there and reasoning in their hearts, 'Why does this man speak that way? He is blaspheming; who can forgive sins but God alone?' Immediately Jesus, aware in His spirit that they were reasoning that way within themselves, said to them, 'Why are you reasoning about these things in your hearts? Which is easier, to say to the paralytic, "Your sins are forgiven"; or to say, "Get up, and pick up your pallet and walk"? But so that you may know that the Son of Man has authority on earth to forgive sins' — He said to the paralytic, 'I say to you, get up, pick up your pallet and go home.' And he got up and immediately picked up the pallet and went out in the sight of everyone, so that they were all amazed and were glorifying God, saying, 'We have never seen anything like this'" (Mk. 2:1-12).

## To Have Authority to Cast out the Demons

"And He went up on the mountain and summoned those whom He Himself wanted, and they came to Him. And He appointed twelve, so that they would be with Him and that He could send them out to preach, and to have authority to cast out the demons. And He appointed the twelve: Simon (to whom He gave the name Peter), and James, the son of Zebedee, and John the brother of James (to them He gave the name Boanerges, which means, 'Sons of Thunder'); and Andrew, and Philip, and Bartholomew, and Matthew, and Thomas, and James the son of Alphaeus, and Thaddaeus, and Simon the Zealot; and Judas Iscariot, who betrayed Him" (Mk. 3:13-19).

## And Gave Them Authority over the Unclean Spirits

"And He summoned the twelve and began to send them out in pairs, and gave them authority over the unclean spirits; and He instructed them that they should take nothing for their journey, except a mere staff—no bread, no bag, no money in their belt—but to wear sandals; and He added, 'Do not put on two tunics.' And He said to them, 'Wherever you enter a house, stay there until you leave town. Any place that does not receive you or listen to you, as you go out from there, shake the dust off the soles of your feet for a testimony against them.' They went out and preached that men should repent. And they were casting out many demons and were anointing with oil many sick people and healing them" (Mk. 6:7-13).

## Their Great Men Exercise Authority over Them

"Hearing this, the ten began to feel indignant with James and John. Calling them to Himself, Jesus said to them, 'You know that those who are recognized as rulers of the Gentiles lord it over them; and their great men exercise authority over them. But it is not this way among you, but whoever wishes to become great among you shall be your servant; and whoever wishes to be first among you shall be slave of all. For even the Son of Man did not come to be served, but to serve, and to give His life a ransom for many'" (Mk. 10:41-45).

## Who Gave You this Authority

"They came again to Jerusalem. And as He was walking in the temple, the chief priests and the scribes and the elders came to Him, and began saying to Him, 'By what authority are You doing these things, or who gave You this authority to do these things?' And Jesus said to them, 'I will ask you one question, and you answer Me, and then I will tell you by what authority I do these things. Was the baptism of John from heaven, or from men? Answer Me.' They began reasoning among themselves, saying, 'If we say,

"From heaven," He will say, "Then why did you not believe him?" But shall we say, "From men"?' — they were afraid of the people, for everyone considered John to have been a real prophet. Answering Jesus, they said, 'We do not know.' And Jesus said to them, 'Nor will I tell you by what authority I do these things'" (Mk. 11:27-33).

## IN THE BOOK OF LUKE

### His Message Was with Authority

"And He came down to Capernaum, a city of Galilee, and He was teaching them on the Sabbath; and they were amazed at His teaching, for His message was with authority. In the synagogue there was a man possessed by the spirit of an unclean demon, and he cried out with a loud voice, 'Let us alone! What business do we have with each other, Jesus of Nazareth? Have You come to destroy us? I know who You are — the Holy One of God!' But Jesus rebuked him, saying, 'Be quiet and come out of him!' And when the demon had thrown him down in the midst of the people, he came out of him without doing him any harm. And amazement came upon them all, and they began talking with one another saying, 'What is this message? For with authority and power He commands the unclean spirits and they come out.' And the report about Him was spreading into every locality in the surrounding district" (Lk. 4:31-37).

## The Son of Man Has Authority on Earth

"One day He was teaching; and there were some Pharisees and teachers of the law sitting there, who had come from every village of Galilee and Judea and from Jerusalem; and the power of the Lord was present for Him to perform healing. And some men were carrying on a bed a man who was paralyzed; and they were trying to bring him in and to set him down in front of Him. But not finding any way to bring him in because of the crowd, they went up on the roof and let him down through the tiles with his stretcher, into the middle of the crowd, in front of Jesus. Seeing their faith, He said, 'Friend, your sins are forgiven you.' The scribes and the Pharisees began to reason, saying, 'Who is this man who speaks blasphemies? Who can forgive sins, but God alone?' But Jesus, aware of their reasonings, answered and said to them, 'Why are you reasoning in your hearts? Which is easier, to say, "Your sins have been forgiven you," or to say, "Get up and walk"? But, so that you may know that the Son of Man has authority on earth to forgive sins,' — He said to the paralytic — 'I say to you, get up, and pick up your stretcher and go home.' Immediately he got up before them, and picked up what he had been lying on, and went home glorifying God. They were all struck with astonishment and began glorifying God; and they were filled with fear, saying, 'We have seen remarkable things today'" (Lk. 5:17-26).

## Placed Under Authority, with Soldiers Under Me

"When He had completed all His discourse in the hearing of the people, He went to Capernaum. And a centurion's slave, who was highly regarded by him, was sick and about to die. When he heard about Jesus, he sent some Jewish elders asking Him to come and save the life of his slave. When they came to Jesus, they earnestly implored Him, saying, 'He is worthy for You to grant this to him; for he loves our nation and it was he who built us our synagogue." Now Jesus started on His way with them; and when He was not far from the house, the centurion sent friends, saying to Him, 'Lord, do not trouble Yourself further, for I am not worthy for You to come under my roof; for this reason I did not even consider myself worthy to come to You, but just say the word, and my servant will be healed. For I also am a man placed under authority, with soldiers under me; and I say to this one, "Go!" and he goes, and to another, "Come!" and he comes, and to my slave, "Do this!" and he does it.' Now when Jesus heard this, He marveled at him, and turned and said to the crowd that was following Him, 'I say to you, not even in Israel have I found such great faith.' When those who had been sent returned to the house, they found the slave in good health" (Lk. 7:1-10).

*Chapter Three*

# Gave them Power and Authority over All the Demons

"And He called the twelve together, and gave them power and authority over all the demons and to heal diseases. And He sent them out to proclaim the kingdom of God and to perform healing. And He said to them, 'Take nothing for your journey, neither a staff, nor a bag, nor bread, nor money; and do not even have two tunics apiece. Whatever house you enter, stay there until you leave that city. And as for those who do not receive you, as you go out from that city, shake the dust off your feet as a testimony against them.' Departing, they began going throughout the villages, preaching the gospel and healing everywhere" (Lk. 9:1-6).

# Given You Authority to Tread on Serpents and Scorpions

"The seventy returned with joy, saying, 'Lord, even the demons are subject to us in Your name.' And He said to them, 'I was watching Satan fall from heaven like lightning. Behold, I have given you authority to tread on serpents and scorpions, and over all the power of the enemy, and nothing will injure you. Nevertheless do not rejoice in this, that the spirits are subject to you, but rejoice that your names are recorded in heaven'" (Lk. 10:17-20).

# He Has Authority to Cast into Hell

"I say to you, My friends, do not be afraid of those who kill the body and after that have no more that they can do. But I will warn you whom to fear: fear the One who, after He has killed, has authority to cast into hell; yes, I tell you, fear Him! Are not five sparrows sold for two cents? Yet not one of them is forgotten before God. Indeed, the very hairs of your head are all numbered. Do not fear; you are more valuable than many sparrows" (Lk. 12:4-7).

# You Are to Be in Authority over Ten Cities

"While they were listening to these things, Jesus went on to tell a parable, because He was near Jerusalem, and they supposed that the kingdom of God was going to appear immediately. So He said, 'A nobleman went to a distant country to receive a kingdom for himself, and then return. And he called ten of his slaves, and gave them ten minas and said to them, "Do business with this until I come back." But his citizens hated him and sent a delegation after him, saying, "We do not want this man to reign over us." When he returned, after receiving the kingdom, he ordered that these slaves, to whom he had given the money, be called to him so that he might know what business they had done. The first appeared, saying, "Master, your mina has made ten minas more." And he said to him, "Well done, good slave, because you have been faithful in a very little thing, you are to be in authority over ten cities." The second came, saying,

'Your mina, master, has made five minas." And he said to him also, "And you are to be over five cities." Another came, saying, "Master, here is your mina, which I kept put away in a handkerchief; for I was afraid of you, because you are an exacting man; you take up what you did not lay down and reap what you did not sow." He said to him, "By your own words I will judge you, you worthless slave. Did you know that I am an exacting man, taking up what I did not lay down and reaping what I did not sow? Then why did you not put my money in the bank, and having come, I would have collected it with interest?" Then he said to the bystanders, "Take the mina away from him and give it to the one who has the ten minas." And they said to him, "Master, he has ten minas already." I tell you that to everyone who has, more shall be given, but from the one who does not have, even what he does have shall be taken away. But these enemies of mine, who did not want me to reign over them, bring them here and slay them in my presence'" (Lk. 19:11-27).

## Who Is the One Who Gave You this Authority?

"On one of the days while He was teaching the people in the temple and preaching the gospel, the chief priests and the scribes with the elders confronted Him, and they spoke, saying to Him, 'Tell us by what authority You are doing these things, or who is the one who gave You this authority?' Jesus answered and said to them, 'I will also ask you a question, and you tell Me: "Was the baptism of John from heaven or from men?" They reasoned among themselves, saying, 'If we say, "From heaven," He will say, "Why did you not believe him?" But if we say, "From men," all the people will stone us to death, for they are convinced that John was a prophet.' So they answered that they did not know where it came from. And Jesus said to them, 'Nor will I tell you by what authority I do these things'" (Lk. 20:1-8).

## The Rule and the Authority of the Governor

"The scribes and the chief priests tried to lay hands on Him that very hour, and they feared the people; for they understood that He spoke this parable against them. So they watched Him, and sent spies who pretended to be righteous, in order that they might catch Him in some statement, so that they could deliver Him to the rule and the authority of the governor. They questioned Him, saying, 'Teacher, we know that You speak and teach correctly, and You are not partial to any, but teach the way of God in truth. Is it lawful for us to pay taxes to Caesar, or not?' But He detected their trickery and said to them, 'Show Me a denarius. Whose likeness and inscription does it have?' They said, 'Caesar's.' And He said to them, 'Then render to Caesar the things that are Caesar's, and to God the things that are God's.' And they were unable to catch Him in a saying in the presence of the people; and being amazed at His answer, they became silent" (Lk. 20:19-26).

## And Those Who Have Authority over Them

"And there arose also a dispute among them as to which one of them was regarded to be greatest. And He said to them, 'The kings of the Gentiles lord it over them; and those who have authority over them are called "Benefactors." But it is not this way with you, but the one who is the greatest among you must become like the youngest, and the leader like the servant. For who is greater, the one who reclines at the table or the one who serves? Is it not the one who reclines at the table? But I am among you as the one who serves'" (Lk. 22:24-27).

# IN THE BOOK OF JOHN

## What Sign Do You Show Us as Your Authority

"The Passover of the Jews was near, and Jesus went up to Jerusalem. And He found in the temple those who were selling oxen and sheep and doves, and the money changers seated at their tables. And He made a scourge of cords, and drove them all out of the temple, with the sheep and the oxen; and He poured out the coins of the money changers and overturned their tables; and to those who were selling the doves He said, 'Take these things away; stop making My Father's house a place of business.' His disciples remembered that it was written, 'ZEAL FOR YOUR HOUSE WILL CONSUME ME.' The Jews then said to Him, 'What sign do You show us as your authority for doing these things?' Jesus answered them, 'Destroy this temple, and in three days I will raise it up.' The Jews then said, 'It took forty-six years to build this temple, and will You raise it up in three days?' But He was speaking of the temple of His body. So when He was raised from the dead, His disciples remembered that He said this; and they believed the Scripture and the word which Jesus had spoken. Now when He was in Jerusalem at the Passover, during the feast, many believed in His name, observing His signs which He was doing. But Jesus, on His part, was not entrusting Himself to them, for He knew all men, and because He did not need anyone to testify concerning man, for He Himself knew what was in man" (Jn. 2:13-25).

## He Gave Him Authority to Execute Judgment

"Truly, truly, I say to you, he who hears My word, and believes Him who sent Me, has eternal life, and does not come into judgment, but has passed out of death into life. Truly, truly, I say to you, an hour is coming and now is, when the dead shall hear the voice of the Son of God; and those who hear shall live. For just as the Father has life in Himself, even so He gave to the Son also to have life in Himself; and He gave Him authority to execute judgment, because He is the Son of Man. Do not marvel at this; for an hour is coming, in which all who are in the tombs shall hear His voice, and shall come forth; those who did the good deeds to a resurrection of life, those who committed the evil deeds to a resurrection of judgment" (Jn. 5:24-29).

## I Have Authority to Lay it Down, and I Have Authority to Take it Up Again

"I am the good shepherd; the good shepherd lays down His life for the sheep. He who is a hireling, and not a shepherd, who is not the owner of the sheep, beholds the wolf coming, and leaves the sheep, and flees, and the wolf snatches them, and scatters them. He flees because he is a hireling, and is not concerned about the sheep. I am the good shepherd; and I know My own, and My own know Me, even as the Father knows Me and I know the Father; and I lay down My life for the sheep. And I have other sheep, which are not of this fold; I must bring them also, and they shall hear My voice; and they shall become one flock with one shepherd. For this reason the Father loves Me, because I lay down My life that I may take it again. No one has taken it away from Me, but I lay it down on My own initiative. I have authority to lay it down, and I have authority to take it up again. This commandment I received from My Father" (Jn. 10:11-18).

## You Gave Him Authority over All Flesh

"These things Jesus spoke; and lifting up His eyes to heaven, He said, 'Father, the hour has come; glorify Thy Son, that the Son may glorify Thee, even as Thou gavest Him authority over all mankind, that to all whom Thou hast given Him, He may give eternal life. And this is eternal life, that they may know Thee, the only true God, and Jesus Christ whom Thou hast sent. I glorified Thee on the earth, having accomplished the work which Thou hast given Me to do. And now, glorify Thou Me together with Thyself, Father, with the glory which I had with Thee before the world was'" (Jn. 17:1-5).

## I Have Authority to Release You

"When Pilate therefore heard this statement, he was the more afraid; and he entered into the Praetorium again, and said to Jesus, 'Where are You from?' But Jesus gave him no answer. Pilate therefore said to Him, 'You do not speak to me? Do You not know that I have authority to release You, and I have authority to crucify You?' Jesus answered, 'You would have no authority over Me, unless it had been given you from above; for this reason he who delivered Me up to you has the greater sin.' As a result of this Pilate made efforts to release Him, but the Jews cried out, saying, 'If you release this Man, you are no friend of Caesar; everyone who makes himself out to be a king opposes Caesar'" (Jn. 19:8-12).

## IN THE BOOK OF ACTS

## The Father Has Fixed by His Own Authority

"And so when they had come together, they were asking Him, saying, 'Lord, is it at this time You are restoring the kingdom to Israel?' He said to them, 'It is not for you to know times or epochs which the Father has fixed by His own authority; but you shall receive power when the Holy Spirit has come upon you; and you shall be My witnesses both in Jerusalem, and in all Judea and Samaria, and even to the remotest part of the earth.' And after He had said these things, He was lifted up while they were looking on, and a cloud received Him out of their sight. And as they were gazing intently into the sky while He was departing, behold, two men in white clothing stood beside them; and they also said, 'Men of Galilee, why do you stand looking into the sky? This Jesus, who has been taken up from you into heaven, will come in just the same way as you have watched Him go into heaven'" (Ac. 1:6-11).

## Give this Authority to Me as Well

"Now when the apostles in Jerusalem heard that Samaria had received the word of God, they sent them Peter and John, who came down and prayed for them, that they might receive the Holy Spirit. For He had not yet fallen upon any of them; they had simply been baptized in the name of the Lord Jesus. Then they began laying their hands on them, and they were receiving the Holy Spirit. Now when Simon saw that the Spirit was bestowed through the laying on of the apostles' hands, he offered them money, saying, 'Give this authority to me as well, so that everyone on whom I lay my hands may receive the Holy Spirit.' But Peter said to him, 'May your silver perish with you, because you thought you could obtain the gift of God with money! You have no part or portion in this matter, for your heart is not right before God.

Therefore repent of this wickedness of yours, and pray the Lord that if possible, the intention of your heart may be forgiven you. For I see that you are in the gall of bitterness and in the bondage of iniquity.' But Simon answered and said, 'Pray to the Lord for me yourselves, so that nothing of what you have said may come upon me'" (Ac. 8:14-24).

## He Has Authority from the Chief Priests

"Now there was a certain disciple at Damascus, named Ananias; and the Lord said to him in a vision, 'Ananias.' And he said, 'Behold, here am I, Lord.' And the Lord said to him, 'Arise and go to the street called Straight, and inquire at the house of Judas for a man from Tarsus named Saul, for behold, he is praying, and he has seen in a vision a man named Ananias come in and lay his hands on him, so that he might regain his sight.' But Ananias answered, 'Lord, I have heard from many about this man, how much harm he did to Thy saints at Jerusalem; and here he has authority from the chief priests to bind all who call upon Thy name.' But the Lord said to him, 'Go, for he is a chosen instrument of Mine, to bear My name before the Gentiles and kings and the sons of Israel; for I will show him how much he must suffer for My name's sake.' And Ananias departed and entered the house, and after laying his hands on him said, 'Brother Saul, the Lord Jesus, who appeared to you on the road by which you were coming, has sent me so that you may regain your sight, and be filled with the Holy Spirit.' And immediately there fell from his eyes something like scales, and he regained his sight, and he arose and was baptized; and he took food and was strengthened. Now for several days he was with the disciples who were at Damascus, and immediately he began to proclaim Jesus in the synagogues, saying, 'He is the Son of God.' And all those hearing him continued to be amazed, and were saying, 'Is this not he who in Jerusalem destroyed those who called on this name, and who had come here for the purpose of bringing them bound before the chief priests?' But Saul kept increasing in strength and confounding the Jews who lived at Damascus by proving that this Jesus is the Christ." (Ac. 9:10-22).

## Received Authority

"So then, I thought to myself that I had to do many things hostile to the name of Jesus of Nazareth. And this is just what I did in Jerusalem; not only did I lock up many of the saints in prisons, having received authority from the chief priests, but also when they were being put to death I cast my vote against them. And as I punished them often in all the synagogues, I tried to force them to blaspheme; and being furiously enraged at them, I kept pursuing them even to foreign cities" (Ac. 26:9-11).

## With the Authority and Commission of the Chief Priests

"While thus engaged as I was journeying to Damascus with the authority and commission of the chief priests, at midday, O King, I saw on the way a light from heaven, brighter than the sun, shining all around me and those who were journeying with me. And when we had all fallen to the ground, I heard a voice saying to me in the Hebrew dialect, 'Saul, Saul, why are you persecuting Me? It is hard for you to kick against the goads.' And I said, 'Who art Thou, Lord?' And the Lord said, 'I am Jesus whom you are persecuting. But arise, and stand on your feet; for this purpose I have appeared to you, to appoint you a minister and a witness not only to the things which you have seen, but also to the things in which I will appear to you; delivering you from the Jewish people and from the Gentiles, to whom I am sending you, to open their eyes so that they may turn from darkness to light and from the dominion of Satan to God, in order that they may receive forgiveness of sins and an inheritance among those who have been sanctified by faith in Me.' (Ac. 26:12-18).

## IN THE BOOK OF ROMANS

### There Is No Authority Except from God

"Let every person be in subjection to the governing authorities. For there is no authority except from God, and those which exist are established by God. Therefore he who resists authority has opposed the ordinance of God; and they who have opposed will receive condemnation upon themselves. For rulers are not a cause of fear for good behavior, but for evil. Do you want to have no fear of authority? Do what is good, and you will have praise from the same; for it is a minister of God to you for good. But if you do what is evil, be afraid; for it does not bear the sword for nothing; for it is a minister of God, an avenger who brings wrath upon the one who practices evil. Wherefore it is necessary to be in subjection, not only because of wrath, but also for conscience' sake. For because of this you also pay taxes, for rulers are servants of God, devoting themselves to this very thing. Render to all what is due them: tax to whom tax is due; custom to whom custom; fear to whom fear; honor to whom honor" (Ro. 13:1-7).

## IN THE BOOK OF 1 CORINTHIANS

### Does Not Have Authority over His Own Body

"Now concerning the things about which you wrote, it is good for a man not to touch a woman. But because of immoralities, let each man have his own wife, and let each woman have her own husband. Let the husband fulfill his duty to his wife, and likewise also the wife to her husband. The wife does not have authority over her own body, but the husband does; and likewise also the husband does not have authority over his own body, but the wife does. Stop depriving one another, except by agreement for a time that you may devote yourselves to prayer, and come together again lest Satan tempt you because of your lack of self-control. But this I say by way of concession, not of command. Yet I wish that all men were even as I myself am. However, each man has his own gift from God, one in this manner, and another in that" (1Co. 7:1-7).

## Being Under No Constraint, but Has Authority

"But if any man thinks that he is acting unbecomingly toward his virgin daughter, if she should be of full age, and if it must be so, let him do what he wishes, he does not sin; let her marry. But he who stands firm in his heart, being under no constraint, but has authority over his own will, and has decided this in his own heart, to keep his own virgin daughter, he will do well. So then both he who gives his own virgin daughter in marriage does well, and he who does not give her in marriage will do better" (1Co. 7:36-38).

## A Symbol of Authority on Her Head

"Now I praise you because you remember me in everything, and hold firmly to the traditions, just as I delivered them to you. But I want you to understand that Christ is the head of every man, and the man is the head of a woman, and God is the head of Christ. Every man who has something on his head while praying or prophesying, disgraces his head. But every woman who has her head uncovered while praying or prophesying, disgraces her head; for she is one and the same with her whose head is shaved. For if a woman does not cover her head, let her also have her hair cut off; but if it is disgraceful for a woman to have her hair cut off or her head shaved, let her cover her head. For a man ought not to have his head covered, since he is the image and glory of God; but the woman is the glory of man. For man does not originate from woman, but woman from man; for indeed man was not created for the woman's sake, but woman for the man's sake. Therefore the woman ought to have a symbol of authority on her head, because of the angels. However, in the Lord, neither is woman independent of man, nor is man independent of woman. For as the woman originates from the man, so also the man has his birth through the woman; and all things originate from God. Judge for yourselves: is it proper for a woman to pray to God with head uncovered? Does not even nature itself teach you that if a man has long hair, it is a dishonor to him, but if a woman has long hair, it is a glory to her? For her hair is given to her for a covering. But if one is inclined to be contentious, we have no other practice, nor have the churches of God" (1Co. 11:2-16).

## He Has Abolished All Rule and All Authority and Power

"But now Christ has been raised from the dead, the first fruits of those who are asleep. For since by a man came death, by a man also came the resurrection of the dead. For as in Adam all die, so also in Christ all shall be made alive. But each in his own order: Christ the first fruits, after that those who are Christ's at His coming, then comes the end, when

He delivers up the kingdom to the God and Father, when He has abolished all rule and all authority and power. For He must reign until He has put all His enemies under His feet. The last enemy that will be abolished is death. For HE HAS PUT ALL THINGS IN SUBJECTION UNDER HIS FEET. But when He says, 'All things are put in subjection,' it is evident that He is excepted who put all things in subjection to Him. And when all things are subjected to Him, then the Son Himself also will be subjected to the One who subjected all things to Him, that God may be all in all" (1Co. 15:20-28).

## IN THE BOOK OF 2 CORINTHIANS

### If I Boast Somewhat Further About Our Authority

"You are looking at things as they are outwardly. If anyone is confident in himself that he is Christ's, let him consider this again within himself, that just as he is Christ's, so also are we. For even if I should boast somewhat further about our authority, which the Lord gave for building you up and not for destroying you, I shall not be put to shame, for I do not wish to seem as if I would terrify you by my letters. For they say, 'His letters are weighty and strong, but his personal presence is unimpressive, and his speech contemptible.' Let such a person consider this, that what we are in word by letters when absent, such persons we are also in deed when present" (2Co. 10:7-11).

*Chapter Three*

## In Accordance with the Authority

"Test yourselves to see if you are in the faith; examine yourselves! Or do you not recognize this about yourselves, that Jesus Christ is in you—unless indeed you fail the test? But I trust that you will realize that we ourselves do not fail the test. Now we pray to God that you do no wrong; not that we ourselves may appear approved, but that you may do what is right, even though we should appear unapproved. For we can do nothing against the truth, but only for the truth. For we rejoice when we ourselves are weak but you are strong; this we also pray for, that you be made complete. For this reason I am writing these things while absent, in order that when present I may not use severity, in accordance with the authority which the Lord gave me, for building up and not for tearing down" (2Co. 13:5-10).

## IN THE BOOK OF EPHESIANS

### Far Above All Rule and Authority and Power

"For this reason I too, having heard of the faith in the Lord Jesus which exists among you, and your love for all the saints, do not cease giving thanks for you, while making mention of you in my prayers; that the God of our Lord Jesus Christ, the Father of glory, may give to you a spirit of wisdom and of revelation in the knowledge of Him. I pray that the eyes of your heart may be enlightened, so that you may know what is the hope of His calling, what are the riches of the glory of His inheritance in the saints, and what is the surpassing greatness of His power toward us who believe. These are in accordance with the working of the strength of His might which He brought about in Christ, when He raised Him from the dead, and seated Him at His right hand in the heavenly places, far above all rule and authority and power and dominion, and every name that is named, not only in this age, but also in the one to come. And He put all things in subjection under His feet, and gave Him as head over all things to the church, which is His body, the fullness of Him who fills all in all" (Eph. 1:15-23).

## IN THE BOOK OF COLOSSIANS

### He Is the Head Over All Rule and Authority

"See to it that no one takes you captive through philosophy and empty deception, according to the tradition of men, according to the elementary principles of the world, rather than according to Christ. For in Him all the fullness of Deity dwells in bodily form, and in Him you have been made complete, and He is the head over all rule and authority; and in Him you were also circumcised with a circumcision made without hands, in the removal of the body of the flesh by the circumcision of Christ; having been buried with Him in baptism, in which you were also raised up with Him through faith in the working of God, who raised Him from the dead. And when you were dead in your transgressions and the uncircumcision of your flesh, He made you alive together with Him, having forgiven us all our transgressions, having canceled out the certificate of debt consisting of decrees against us and which was hostile to us; and He has taken it out of the way, having nailed it to the cross. When He had disarmed the rulers and authorities, He made a public display of them, having triumphed over them through Him" (Col. 2:8-15).

## IN THE BOOK OF 1 THESSALONIANS

### We Might Have Asserted Our Authority

"For you yourselves know, brethren, that our coming to you was not in vain, but after we had already suffered and been mistreated in Philippi, as you know, we had the boldness in our God to speak to you the gospel of God amid much opposition. For our exhortation does not come from error or impurity or by way of deceit; but just as we have been approved by God to be entrusted with the gospel, so we speak, not as pleasing men but God, who examines our hearts. For we never came with flattering speech, as you know, nor with a pretext for greed—God is witness—nor did we seek glory from men, either from you or from others, even though as apostles of Christ we might have asserted our authority. But we proved to be gentle among you, as a nursing mother tenderly cares for her own children. Having thus a fond affection for you, we were well-pleased to impart to you not only the gospel of God but also our own lives, because you had become very dear to us" (1Th. 2:1-8).

## By the Authority of the Lord Jesus

"Finally then, brethren, we request and exhort you in the Lord Jesus, that, as you received from us instruction as to how you ought to walk and please God (just as you actually do walk), that you may excel still more. For you know what commandments we gave you by the authority of the Lord Jesus. For this is the will of God, your sanctification; that is, that you abstain from sexual immorality; that each of you know how to possess his own vessel in sanctification and honor, not in lustful passion, like the Gentiles who do not know God; and that no man transgress and defraud his brother in the matter because the Lord is the avenger in all these things, just as we also told you before and solemnly warned you. For God has not called us for the purpose of impurity, but in sanctification. Consequently, he who rejects this is not rejecting man but the God who gives His Holy Spirit to you" (1Th. 4:1-8).

## IN THE BOOK OF 1 TIMOTHY

## For Kings and All Who are in Authority

"First of all, then, I urge that entreaties and prayers, petitions and thanksgivings, be made on behalf of all men, for kings and all who are in authority, in order that we may lead a tranquil and quiet life in all godliness and dignity. This is good and acceptable in the sight of God our Savior, who desires all men to be saved and to come to the knowledge of the truth. For there is one God, and one mediator also between God and men, the man Christ Jesus, who gave Himself as a ransom for all, the testimony borne at the proper time. And for this I was appointed a preacher and an apostle (I am telling the truth, I am not lying) as a teacher of the Gentiles in faith and truth" (1Ti. 2:1-7).

## Authority over a Man

"Therefore I want the men in every place to pray, lifting up holy hands, without wrath and dissension. Likewise, I want women to adorn themselves with proper clothing, modestly and discreetly, not with braided hair and gold or pearls or costly garments; but rather by means of good works, as befits women making a claim to godliness. Let a woman quietly receive instruction with entire submissiveness. But I do not allow a woman to teach or exercise authority over a man, but to remain quiet. For it was Adam who was first created, and then Eve. And it was not Adam who was deceived, but the woman being quite deceived, fell into transgression. But women shall be preserved through the bearing of children if they continue in faith and love and sanctity with self-restraint" (1Ti. 2:8-15).

*Chapter Three*

# IN THE BOOK OF TITUS

## Exhort and Reprove with All Authority

"These things speak and exhort and reprove with all authority. Let no one disregard you" (Tit. 2:15).

# IN THE BOOK OF 1 PETER

## The One in Authority

"Submit yourselves for the Lord's sake to every human institution, whether to a king as the one in authority, or to governors as sent by him for the punishment of evildoers and the praise of those who do right. For such is the will of God that by doing right you may silence the ignorance of foolish men. Act as free men, and do not use your freedom as a covering for evil, but use it as bondslaves of God. Honor all men; love the brotherhood, fear God, honor the king" (1Pe. 2:13-17).

# IN THE BOOK OF 2 PETER

## Who Indulge the Flesh in its Corrupt Desires and Despise Authority

"For if God did not spare angels when they sinned, but cast them into hell and committed them to pits of darkness, reserved for judgment; and did not spare the ancient world, but preserved Noah, a preacher of righteousness, with seven others, when He brought a flood upon the world of the ungodly; and if He condemned the cities of Sodom and Gomorrah to destruction by reducing them to ashes, having made them an example to those who would live ungodly thereafter; and if He rescued righteous Lot, oppressed by the sensual conduct of unprincipled men (for by what he saw and heard that righteous man, while living among them, felt his righteous soul tormented day after day with their lawless deeds), then the Lord knows how to rescue the godly from temptation, and to keep the unrighteous under punishment for the day of judgment, and especially those who indulge the flesh in its corrupt desires and despise authority. Daring, self-willed, they do not tremble when they revile angelic majesties, whereas angels who are greater in might and power do not bring a reviling judgment against them before the Lord. But these, like unreasoning animals, born as creatures of instinct to be captured and killed, reviling where they have no knowledge, will in the destruction of those creatures also be destroyed, suffering wrong as the wages of doing wrong. They count it a pleasure to revel in the daytime. They are stains and blemishes, reveling in their deceptions, as they carouse with you, having eyes full of adultery and that never cease from sin, enticing unstable souls, having a heart trained in greed, accursed children; forsaking the right way they have gone astray, having followed the way of Balaam, the son of Beor, who loved the wages of unrighteousness, but he received a rebuke for his own transgression; for a dumb donkey, speaking with a voice of a man, restrained the madness of the prophet" (2Pe. 2:4-16).

## IN THE BOOK OF JUDE

### Reject Authority, and Revile Angelic Majesties

"Yet in the same manner these men, also by dreaming, defile the flesh, and reject authority, and revile angelic majesties. But Michael the archangel, when he disputed with the devil and argued about the body of Moses, did not dare pronounce against him a railing judgment, but said, 'The Lord rebuke you.' But these men revile the things which they do not understand; and the things which they know by instinct, like unreasoning animals, by these things they are destroyed. Woe to them! For they have gone the way of Cain, and for pay they have rushed headlong into the error of Balaam, and perished in the rebellion of Korah. These men are those who are hidden reefs in your love feasts when they feast with you without fear, caring for themselves; clouds without water, carried along by winds; autumn trees without fruit, doubly dead, uprooted; wild waves of the sea, casting up their own shame like foam; wandering stars, for whom the black darkness has been reserved forever" (Jude 1:8-13).

*Chapter Three*

# Our Lord, be Glory, Majesty, Dominion and Authority

"Now to Him who is able to keep you from stumbling, and to make you stand in the presence of His glory blameless with great joy, to the only God our Savior, through Jesus Christ our Lord, be glory, majesty, dominion and authority, before all time and now and forever. Amen" (Jude 1:24-25).

## IN THE BOOK OF REVELATION

## I Also Have Received Authority from My Father

"I know your deeds, and your love and faith and service and perseverance, and that your deeds of late are greater than at first. But I have this against you, that you tolerate the woman Jezebel, who calls herself a prophetess, and she teaches and leads My bond-servants astray, so that they commit acts of immorality and eat things sacrificed to idols. And I gave her time to repent; and she does not want to repent of her immorality. Behold, I will cast her upon a bed of sickness, and those who commit adultery with her into great tribulation, unless they repent of her deeds. And I will kill her children with pestilence; and all the churches will know that I am He who searches the minds and hearts; and I will give to each one of you according to your deeds. But I say to you, the rest who are in Thyatira, who do not hold this teaching, who have not known the deep things of Satan, as they call them—I place no other burden on you. Nevertheless what you have, hold fast until I come. And he who overcomes, and he who keeps My deeds until the end, TO HIM I WILL GIVE AUTHORITY OVER THE NATIONS; AND HE SHALL RULE THEM WITH A ROD OF IRON, AS THE VESSELS OF THE POTTER ARE BROKEN TO PIECES, as I also have received authority from My Father; and I will give him the morning star. He who has an ear, let him hear what the Spirit says to the churches" (Rev. 2:19-29).

## Authority Was Given to Them

"And when He broke the fourth seal, I heard the voice of the fourth living creature saying, 'Come.' And I looked, and behold, an ashen horse; and he who sat on it had the name Death; and Hades was following with him. And authority was given to them over a fourth of the earth, to kill with sword and with famine and with pestilence and by the wild beasts of the earth" (Rev. 6:7-8).

## I Will Grant Authority to My Two Witnesses

"And there was given me a measuring rod like a staff; and someone said, 'Rise and measure the temple of God, and the altar, and those who worship in it. And leave out the court which is outside the temple, and do not measure it, for it has been given to the nations; and they will tread under foot the holy city for forty-two months. And I will grant authority to my two witnesses, and they will prophesy for twelve hundred and sixty days, clothed in sackcloth. These are the two olive trees and the two lampstands that stand before the Lord of the earth. And if anyone desires to harm them, fire proceeds out of their mouth and devours their enemies; and if anyone would desire to harm them, in this manner he must be killed. These have the power to shut up the sky, in order that rain may not fall during the days of their prophesying; and they have power over the waters to turn them into blood, and to smite the earth with every plague, as often as they desire'" (Rev. 11:1-6).

## The Authority of His Christ Have Come

"And there was war in heaven, Michael and his angels waging war with the dragon. And the dragon and his angels waged war, and they were not strong enough, and there was no longer a place found for them in heaven. And the great dragon was thrown down, the serpent of old who is called the devil and Satan, who deceives the whole world; he was thrown down to the earth, and his angels were thrown down with him. And I heard a loud voice in heaven, saying, 'Now the salvation, and the power, and the kingdom of our God and the authority of His Christ have come, for the accuser of our brethren has been thrown down, who accuses them before our God day and night. And they overcame him because of the blood of the Lamb and because of the word of their testimony, and they did not love their life even to death. For this reason, rejoice, O heavens and you who dwell in them. Woe to the earth and the sea, because the devil has come down to you, having great wrath, knowing that he has only a short time'" (Rev. 12:7-12).

## His Throne and Great Authority

"And he stood on the sand of the seashore. And I saw a beast coming up out of the sea, having ten horns and seven heads, and on his horns were ten diadems, and on his heads were blasphemous names. And the beast which I saw was like a leopard, and his feet were like those of a bear, and his mouth like the mouth of a lion. And the dragon gave him his power and his throne and great authority. And I saw one of his heads as if it had been slain, and his fatal wound was healed. And the whole earth was amazed and followed after the beast; and they worshiped the dragon, because he gave his authority to the beast; and they worshiped the beast, saying, 'Who is like the beast, and who is able to wage war with him?' And there was given to him a mouth speaking arrogant words and blasphemies; and authority to act for forty-two months was given to him. And he opened his mouth in blasphemies against God, to blaspheme His name and His tabernacle, that is, those who dwell in heaven" (Rev. 13:1-6).

## Authority Over Every Tribe and People and Tongue and Nation Was Given to Him

"And it was given to him to make war with the saints and to overcome them; and authority over every tribe and people and tongue and nation was given to him. And all who dwell on the earth will worship him, everyone whose name has not been written from the foundation of the world in the book of life of the Lamb who has been slain. If anyone has an ear, let him hear. If anyone is destined for captivity, to captivity he goes; if anyone kills with the sword, with the sword he must be killed. Here is the perseverance and the faith of the saints" (Rev. 13:7-10).

## He Exercises All the Authority

"And I saw another beast coming up out of the earth; and he had two horns like a lamb, and he spoke as a dragon. And he exercises all the authority of the first beast in his presence. And he makes the earth and those who dwell in it to worship the first beast, whose fatal wound was healed. And he performs great signs, so that he even makes fire come down out of heaven to the earth in the presence of men. And he deceives those who dwell on the earth because of the signs which it was given him to perform in the presence of the beast, telling those who dwell on the earth to make an image to the beast who *had the wound of the sword and has come to life. And there was given to him to give breath to the image of the beast, that the image of the beast might even speak and cause as many as do not worship the image of the beast to be killed. And he causes all, the small and the great, and the rich and the poor, and the free men and the slaves, to be given a mark on their right hand, or on their forehead, and he provides that no one should be able to buy or to sell, except the one who has the mark, either the name of the beast or the number of his name. Here is wisdom. Let him who has understanding calculate the number of the beast, for the number is that of a man; and his number is six hundred and sixty-six" (Rev. 13:11-18).

## They Receive Authority as Kings

"The beast that you saw was and is not, and is about to come up out of the abyss and to go to destruction. And those who dwell on the earth will wonder, whose name has not been written in the book of life from the foundation of the world, when they see the beast, that he was and is not and will come. Here is the mind which has wisdom. The seven heads are seven mountains on which the woman sits, and they are seven kings; five have fallen, one is, the other has not yet come; and when he comes, he must remain a little while. And the beast which was and is not, is himself also an eighth, and is one of the seven, and he goes to destruction. And the ten horns which you saw are ten kings, who have not yet received a kingdom, but they receive authority as kings with the beast for one hour. These have one purpose and they give their power and authority to the beast. These will wage war against the Lamb, and the Lamb will overcome them, because He is Lord of lords and King of kings, and those who are with Him are the called and chosen and faithful" (Rev. 17:8-14).

*Chapter Three*

## Having Great Authority

"After these things I saw another angel coming down from heaven, having great authority, and the earth was illumined with his glory. And he cried out with a mighty voice, saying, 'Fallen, fallen is Babylon the great! And she has become a dwelling place of demons and a prison of every unclean spirit, and a prison of every unclean and hateful bird. For all the nations have drunk of the wine of the passion of her immorality, and the kings of the earth have committed acts of immorality with her, and the merchants of the earth have become rich by the wealth of her sensuality'" (Rev. 18:1-3).

# DAILY FAITH CONFESSIONS

(These are not direct quotations from the Bible but are paraphrased confessions based on scripture.)
**SAY THEM OUT LOUD.**

I am God's child (Jn. 1:12). I am royalty (1 Pet. 2:9). I am hidden with Christ in God (Col. 3:3). I am united with the Lord (1 Cor. 6:17). I am a friend of Christ (Jn. 15:15). I am raised up with Him, and seated with Him in heavenly places in Christ Jesus (Eph. 2:6). I was bought with a price (1 Cor. 6:19-20). I am blessed when I come in, and blessed shall I be when I go out (Deut. 28:6). I am a personal witness of Christ (Acts 1:8). I am a saint who prays in the Holy Spirit to keep myself in the love of God (Jude 1:20-21). I draw near with confidence to the throne of grace (Heb. 4:16). I have been adopted by the Father (Eph. 1:5). I am the salt and light of the earth (Mt. 5:13). I am the head and not the tail, and I am above, and not underneath (Deut. 28:13). I have authority to trample serpents and scorpions and over all the power of the enemy (Lk. 10:19). I am a member of the body of Christ (1 Cor. 12:27). God blessed me to be fruitful, and multiply, and replenish the earth, and subdue it: and have dominion (Gen. 1:28). I cannot be separated from God's love (Ro. 8:39). The good work God has begun in me will be perfected (Phil. 1:5). I can do all things through Christ who strengthens me (Phil. 4:13). No weapon that is formed against me will prosper (Is. 54:17). So then faith cometh by hearing, and hearing by the word of God (Ro. 10:17 KJV). Faith is my currency to operate in the kingdom of God (Ro. 14:23). I am God's workmanship created in Christ Jesus for good works, which God prepared beforehand (Eph. 2:10). I have been appointed to bear fruit, and that my fruit would remain (Jn. 15:16). I am being wise when I am winning souls for King Jesus (Pr. 11:30). My body is the temple of the Holy Spirit (1 Cor. 6:19). I have access to God through the Holy Spirit (Eph. 2:18). I have been justified (Ro. 5:1). Therefore there is now no condemnation for those who are in Christ Jesus (Ro. 8:1). Greater is He who is in me than he who is in the world (1 Jn. 4:4). I will do greater works than Jesus because He went to the Father (Jn. 14:12). As God was with Moses, He will be with me; God will not fail me or forsake me (Jos. 1:5). I see myself the way God see me. God sees me as a king (Gen, 17:6, Rev. 1:6) God sees me as royalty (1 Pet. 2:9). God sees me as the righteousness of God in Christ, bold as a lion (Ro. 3:22, Pr. 28:1). God sees me without spot or wrinkle because of the blood of Jesus (1 Pet. 1:19). I am having faith for big things because God owns everything and I'm His son (Ps. 24:1). No man will be able to stand before me all the days of my life (Jos. 1:5). My Father is glorified by this that I bear much fruit, and proves I'm a disciple (see Jn. 15:8). I think big and confess big things because God is big (Ps. 24:1). I will respect God for the big God that He is and my mouth will create whatever I want (Lk. 6:45). I no longer think of millions, my renewed mind thinks of billions because the wealth of the wicked is laid up for the righteous (Pr. 13:22). The sinner's job is to gather and collect for the one who is good in God's sight (Ecc. 2:26). Redemption is not complete without prosperity. Jesus hung on the cross so I can have the whole package, not just salvation (2 Cor. 8:9). I don't have to qualify, Jesus has qualified me. Jesus reversed the curse. The devil is a liar, and Jesus is the Messiah. Jesus is made unto to me wisdom, righteousness, sanctification, and redemption (1 Cor. 1:30). I submit to God, I resist the devil and he flees from me (Jas. 4:7). For God has not given me the spirit of fear; but of power, and of love, and of a sound mind (2 Tim. 1:7). The Holy Spirit will teach me all things (Jn. 14:26). The Holy Spirit will guide me into all truth (Jn.16:13). The Holy Spirit abides in me, and I don't need anyone to teach me, but the anointing teaches me all things (1 Jn. 2:27). I quench fiery darts from the wicked one with the shield of faith (Eph. 6:16). I stand firm against the schemes of the devil (Eph. 6:11). I already have the victory and Satan cannot back me up. I hold my position of consistent victory after victory (2 Cor. 2:14). I walk in love and live by faith (Gal. 5:6). I have been redeemed from the curse of the law, poverty, sickness, and spiritual death (Gal. 3:13; Deut. 28). I will bear so much fruit. I'm God's workmanship created beforehand for good works (Eph. 2:10). God's favor is on my life (Ps. 3:8). God blesses me and His favor surrounds me as with a shield (Ps. 5:12). The kingdom of God is within me (Lk. 17:21). I have a production plant inside of me that bears fruit to change the world (Gen. 1:28). God gives me power to get wealth to establish His covenant on earth (Deut. 8:18). I am blessed to be a blessing (Gen. 12:2). I have Satan on the run. I will make a mockery of him (Jas. 4:7). I'm spending forever with King Jesus (2 Cor. 5:8). Thank you Father for Your love.

# PRAYER FOR SALVATION

## Say the following prayer out loud.

Heavenly Father, I am a sinner and I need a Savior. I confess Jesus Christ as the Lord of my life. I repent of all my sins. Father, I truly believe you raised Jesus from the dead. Father, give me spiritual hunger to spend time in Your Word day and night so my mind is renewed. I understand that by meditating and submitting to Your Word daily I will be transformed into the image of Jesus, day-by-day. Thank you, Father, for Your goodness, mercy, and grace. I pray in Jesus' name. Amen.

## PRAYER FOR BAPTISM OF THE HOLY SPIRIT

Father, I am your child because Jesus is my Lord. Jesus said, "How much more shall your heavenly Father give the Holy Spirit to those who ask Him." I ask you now in the name of Jesus to fill me with the Holy Spirit. Thank you, Father, I received the baptism of the Holy Spirit by faith. I yield my vocal organs and expect to speak in tongues as the Holy Spirit gives me utterance in Jesus name. Father, I plan to pray in the Holy Spirit building myself up on my most holy faith, and keep myself in the love of God, as mentioned in Jude 20 and 21. In Jesus name I decree it. Amen.

# ABOUT THE AUTHOR

Eugene Carvalho is the founder of Receiving by Faith. He is an administrator and Christian author of seventy books. God uses him in the offices of pastor, evangelist and prophet. He holds a bachelor's degree in biblical studies and a double minor in pastoral ministry and world missions. He also holds a master's degree in practical theology. Eugene prayed for a translator and God sent his wife Mercedes who has a six-year degree in Spanish from a university in Tampico, Mexico. They have participated in evangelism in the streets of Mexico for many years. They have also traveled to churches all over the United States and Mexico winning souls and preaching faith. Their current ministry website is: www.receivingbyfaith.org.

# BOOKS BY EUGENE IN ENGLISH

To purchase other books by Eugene Carvalho visit receivingbyfaith.org or amazon.com.

Receiving by Faith
Faith for Every Day: 365 Daily Devotions
Faith Cometh by Hearing, and Hearing by the Word of God
Faith, Hope, and Love
Walk in Love and Live by Faith
Topical Christian Handbook and Scripture Guide
The Gospel Is the Power of God unto Salvation
Seed Time and Harvest Time
Your New Identity in Christ
The Cross and the Blood
The Holy Spirit
The Attributes of God
The Favor of God
The Glory of God
The Grace of God
The Power of God
The Promises of God
The Throne of God
The New Testament Church
Vengeance and Recompense
God's Angel's
Prayer and Fasting
God's Mighty Prophets
A Survey of Jesus Through the Epistles
The Names of Jesus
The Psalms of David
The Righteous Will Flourish like The Palm Tree

# BOOKS BY EUGENE IN SPANISH

Las Promesas de Dios
Los Salmos de David
Lo Sobrenatural: Lo que la Bíblia Tiene que Decir
Una Mirada Topica Del Libro De Los Salmos
Dios es Amor: Lo que la Biblia Tiene que Decir
La Adquisición de la Sabiduría es Vital: Lo que la
Biblia Tiene que Decir

# NOTES

# NOTES

# NOTES